Mammals
WHAT IS AN ANIMAL?

Ted O'Hare

Rourke
Publishing LLC
Vero Beach, Florida 32964

www.rourkepublishing.com

PHOTO CREDITS: All photos © Lynn M. Stone

Title page: Bison gather on the prairie of Wind Cave National Park, South Dakota.

Editor: Frank Sloan

Cover and interior design by Nicola Stratford

Library of Congress Cataloging-in-Publication Data

O'Hare, Ted, 1961-
    Mammals / Ted O'Hare.
        p. cm. -- (What is an animal?)
    Includes bibliographical references and index.
    ISBN 1-59515-420-5 (hardcover)
    1. Mammals--Juvenile literature. I. Title. II. Series: O'Hare, Ted,
1961-   What is an animal?
    QL706.2.O38 2006
    599--dc22

Printed in the USA

CG/CG

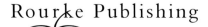

Rourke Publishing

www.rourkepublishing.com – sales@rourkepublishing.com
Post Office Box 3328, Vero Beach, FL 32964
1-800-394-7055

Table of Contents

Mammals

Mammals are one of the **vertebrate** groups of animals. This means they have backbones. Amphibians, reptiles, and birds are also mammals. So are human beings.

Mammals form a group of **warm-blooded** animals. Most mammals have four limbs and give birth to live young. They also produce milk to feed their young. And they have at least some hair or fur.

Mammals, like this giant panda, have hair or fur.

Mammal Habits

Mammals hunt for food. They look for places to sleep and they search for mates. Sometimes they fight and sometimes they play.

Some mammals take long journeys called **migrations**. They look for new sources of food and shelter. A few mammals **hibernate**. They spend winter in a deep sleep. Brown bears and woodchucks hibernate.

African wildebeest migrate to find better food.

Kinds of Mammals

There are about 4,000 kinds, or **species**, of mammals. Scientists divide them into 18 or 19 groups. Rodents, with 1,800 kinds, make up the largest group. Rats, mice, squirrels, and beavers are rodents.

Another group is made up of meat-eaters. Dogs, cats, otters, seals, and bears are some of them. Bats are a large group of flying mammals.

The koala of Australia is a mammal.

Where Mammals Live

Whales and seals live in oceans. Mammals with hoofs live in grasslands. These include zebras and bison. The lynx and pine squirrel live in forests. Kangaroo mice live in deserts.

Places where mammals live are known as their **habitats**. Some mammals live in homes that they have built.

The beaver is a builder. It builds a home next to a stream or lake.

Some mammals, like this tiger, are active in cold weather as well as warm.

A mother grizzly protects her young cub.

Mammal Bodies

Mammals range in size from tiny to huge. It takes 14 hog-nosed bats to weigh just one pound (457 grams). A blue whale, however, can weigh up to 440,000 pounds (199,583 kilograms).

Bats have unusual bodies. Their two front limbs are wings with tiny hands.

Seagoing mammals have streamlined bodies with flippers.

Amazing Mammals

The cheetah is the fastest mammal. It can run nearly 70 miles (112 kilometers) per hour! Sea otters and chimpanzees can use rocks and sticks as simple tools.

Marsupials, like koalas, take care of their babies by protecting them in pouches. The echidna and platypus are mammals that lay eggs.

DiD YOU KNOW?

The elephant seal can dive a mile deep in the ocean. It can stay underwater for 90 minutes!

The echidna is one of only three mammals that lay eggs.

Predator and Prey

Meat-eating mammals are **predators**. They hunt other animals, their **prey**, for food. Most mammals live on a diet of plants. Black bears and raccoons eat both plants and animals. Some small mammals live almost entirely on insects. Most bats, moles, and shrews are insect-eaters.

DID YOU KNOW?

The largest land predator is the Alaskan brown bear. It can weigh as much as 1,500 pounds (682 kilograms).

A Canada lynx catches its favorite prey, a snowshoe hare.

Baby Mammals

Baby mammals may be helpless at birth. Or they may be ready to run. Baby bears and opossums are both helpless and hairless. A baby elk can, however, run with its mother soon after birth.

Mammals grow at first by drinking their mother's milk. At least one parent guides the baby as it grows. A bear cub may spend three or more years at its mother's side.

A sea otter will take care of its baby until it is old enough to care for itself.

People and Mammals

Many people enjoy watching and studying mammals. Farm mammals are important to people. They are a source of milk, food, and clothing. Some farm animals perform work.

Mammals in the wild help keep the balance between predator and prey. They disappear, however, when people destroy their habitats. Many mammals are **endangered**.

GLOSSARY

endangered (en DAYN jerd) — in danger of no longer existing; very rare

habitats (HAB uh tatz) — special kinds of places where animals live, such as a cypress swamp

hibernate (HY ber nayt) — to enter into a deep winter sleep

marsupials (mahr SU pi ulz) — a family of mammals in which mothers raise their young in a pouch

migrations (my GRAY shunz) — travels to distant places at the same time each year

predators (PRED uh terz) — animals that hunt other animals for food

prey (PRAY) — an animal that is hunted by other animals for food

species (SPEE sheez) — within a group of closely related animals, one certain kind, such as a brown bear

vertebrate (VER tuh BRAYT) — an animal with a backbone; fish, amphibians, reptiles, birds, and mammals are vertebrates

warm-blooded (WARM BLUD ed) — refers to birds and mammals, animals whose bodies keep a warm, steady temperature even in cold weather

Index

Further Reading

Arlon, Penelope. *DK First Animal Encyclopedia*. Dorling Kindersley, 2004
Pascoe, Elaine. *Animals with Backbones*. Powerkids Press, 2003
Solway, Andrew. *Classifying Mammals*. Heinemann Library, 2003

Websites to Visit

http://www.biologybrowser.org
http://www.kidport.com/RefLib/Science/Animals/AnimalIndexV.htm

About the Author

Ted O'Hare is an author and editor of children's books. He divides his time between New York City and a home upstate.